# My First Reconciliation

Place my picture here.

_____

(name)

_____

(date)

**at**

_____

(name of church)

# Celebrating Our Faith

## Reconciliation

Principal Program Consultant
Dr. Jane Marie Osterholt, SP

**BROWN-ROA**
*A Division of Harcourt Brace & Company*

**Nihil Obstat**
Rev. Richard L. Schaefer

**Imprimatur**
✠ Most Rev. Jerome Hanus, OSB
Archbishop of Dubuque
August 1, 1998
Feast of Saint Alphonsus Liguori
Patron of Confessors

> The Ad Hoc Committee to Oversee the Use of the Catechism, National Conference of Catholic Bishops, has found this catechetical series to be in conformity with the *Catechism of the Catholic Church.*

The nihil obstat and imprimatur are official declarations that a book or pamphlet is free of doctrinal or moral error. No implication is contained herein that those who granted the nihil obstat and imprimatur agree with the contents, opinions, or statements expressed.

**BROWN-ROA**
*A Division of Harcourt Brace & Company*

### Our Mission

The primary mission of BROWN-ROA is to provide the Catholic markets with the highest quality catechetical print and media resources. The content of these resources reflects the best insights of current theology, methodology, and pedagogical research. These resources are practical and easy to use, designed to meet expressed market needs, and written to reflect the teachings of the Catholic Church.

**Photography Credits**
**Cover:** Stained-glass windows at Zimmerman Chapel, United Theological Seminary, Dayton, Ohio. Photography by Andy Snow Photographics.
**Gene Plaisted/The Crosiers:** 11, 18, 63(c); **Digital Imaging Group:** 10(bl), 14, 15, 19, 23, 26, 34, 35, 38, 38, 42, 51, 51, 59, 62(c), 63(bl), 63(tl), 64(bl), 64(c); **FPG International:** Bill Losh: 30; Telegraph Colour Library: 6; **Jack Holtel:** 27; **PhotoEdit:** Tony Freeman: 22; David Young-Wolff: 46; **Andy Snow Photographics:** 10(c), 39, 43, 47, 50, 61, 62, 64(tl); **Tony Stone Images:** Stewart Cohen: 31; Peter Poulides: 7. Special thanks to the parish communities at St. Charles Borromeo, Kettering; St. Paul's, Oakwood; and Holy Angels, Dayton, for cooperation with photography.

**Illustration Credits**
**Biblical Art: Chris Vallo/The Mazer Corporation:** 8–9, 16–17, 24–25, 32–33, 40–41, 48–49;
**Children's art:** 12–13, 20–21, 28–29, 44–45, 52–53 (prepared by Chelsea Arney, Lisol Arney, Kaley Bartosik, Hannah Berry, Noah Berry, Morgan Brickley, Brittany King, Cecily King, Jackie Malone, Katie Malone, Bob Ninneman, Claudia Ninneman, Erica Ninneman, Laura Grace Ninneman, Brittany Smith, Lauren Vallo, Ryan Vallo, and the art classes of Holy Angels School, Dayton)

Printed in the United States of America

ISBN 0-15-950458-9

10  9  8  7  6  5  4  3  2  1

# Celebrating Our Faith

## Reconciliation

# My First Reconciliation

I will celebrate
the Sacrament of Reconciliation
for the first time
on

_____
(date)

at

_____.
(name of church)

I ask my family, my godparents,
my teacher, my classmates, my friends,
and everyone in my parish community
to help me prepare for this celebration.

_____
(signed)

Here are the signatures of people who are helping
me prepare for my First Reconciliation.

# A Blessing for Beginnings

*"The Lord is merciful! He is kind and patient, and his love never fails."*

—*Psalm 103:8*

**Leader:** Today we gather to begin your journey
toward First Reconciliation.
We are ready to learn from one another
and from our Church community.
And so we pray:
God our Father, show us your mercy and love.
Jesus, Son of God, deliver us from the power of sin.
Holy Spirit, help us grow in charity, justice,
and peace.

**Reader:** Listen to God's message to us:
*(Read Ephesians 2:4–10.)*
The word of the Lord.

**All:** **Thanks be to God.**

**Leader:** We ask God's blessing on our journey together.

**All:** **Holy Trinity, live in our hearts.**
**Teach us to love and forgive.**
**Help us turn to you in true sorrow for sin,**
**and trust in your never-ending mercy.**
**We pray in the words that Jesus taught us.**
***(Pray the Lord's Prayer.)***

**Leader:** May the Lord be with us, now and always.

**All:** **Amen!**

# CHAPTER 1

# WE BELONG

Dear God—Father, Son, and Holy Spirit—you have called us to be Christian. Help us always remain close to you. Amen!

Where do you belong? The people you share important times with and feel at home with are your **community**. Everyone needs to be part of a community. You weren't made to live alone in the world.

Your family is a community. So is your group of friends. You belong to another important community, too. You belong to the **Catholic** Church.

Your Catholic community comes together to worship God at Mass. You celebrate the **sacraments** together. With other Catholic children you learn about God.

You may not know it, but your Catholic community is much bigger than the people you see at church on Sunday. The Church is a family as big as the whole world.

# We Are God's Children

Saint Paul traveled to Greece to tell people about Jesus. In the city of Athens, Paul stood up in the marketplace.

"People of Athens!" Paul said. "I see that you worship many gods. Well, today I am going to tell you about the one true God so that you can come to know him."

Paul pointed to the blue sky. "God made all things. He made the sun and the moon and the stars. He gives life and breath to every person."

People began to listen closely. They wanted to know more.

"God made us all to be one family," Paul continued. "We are God's children, and he wants each of us to turn to him with love."

"How do you know these things?" someone asked.

Paul smiled. "God the Father sent his own Son, Jesus, to tell us all," he said. "Until now many people didn't know how much God loved them, so they turned away from him and sinned. But now everyone knows how strong God's love is. God the Father even raised Jesus from death!"

Some people laughed at Paul. But others believed him. They turned to God and became followers of Jesus.

—based on Acts 17:16–34

# Sacraments of Initiation

Like the people who listened to Saint Paul, we became members of the Church by being baptized. In the Sacrament of **Baptism**, we become part of the Body of Christ.

But there is more to becoming a member of the Catholic community than being baptized. Baptism is the first of three Sacraments of Initiation. The word **initiation** means "becoming a member."

Confirmation is the second Sacrament of Initiation. In Confirmation we receive the Holy Spirit in a special way. We are joined even more closely to the Church community.

The third Sacrament of Initiation is the **Eucharist**. Of course, we celebrate the Eucharist every Sunday by taking part in the Mass. But when we receive Jesus in Holy Communion for the first time, we complete our initiation. First Communion makes us fully members of the Church because it joins us completely with Jesus and with one another.

## We Ask

**Why aren't the three Sacraments of Initiation always celebrated at the same time?**

Early Christians were baptized, confirmed, and received into Eucharistic communion all at once. The same is true today for many adults and children of school age and for infants in the Eastern Rites of the Church. In the Latin Rite, Catholics baptized as infants usually receive First Communion around the age of seven and may celebrate Confirmation at that time or some time later.
(Catechism, #1229–1233)

## I Am a Catholic

Fill in the blanks to finish the baptismal certificate. In the space, draw or glue a picture of your Baptism.

**I was baptized on**

_____

at _____ **Church.**

**My godparents are**

_____

**and**

_____.

# Children of One Family

We thank God for making us members of one family through the Sacraments of Initiation.

God, our loving Father,
because you love us,
you sent Jesus, your Son,
to bring us to you
and to gather us around him
as the children of one family.
**Hosanna in the highest!**
Jesus came to show us
how we could love you, Father,
by loving one another.
He came to take away sin and hate,
which keeps us from being friends,
and which makes us all unhappy.
**Hosanna in the highest!**
He promised to send the Holy Spirit,
to be with us always
so that we can live as your children.
**Hosanna in the highest!**
—*based on Eucharistic Prayer II for Children*

# Chapter 2
# We Celebrate God's Love

**D**ear God—Father, Son, and Holy Spirit—you are always ready to welcome us back. Help us turn to you with love and faithfulness. Amen!

Even in the most loving families, people do not always act lovingly. Even best friends sometimes hurt each other.

You know what it is like to do something wrong or hurt someone else. And you know what it is like to feel sorry and want to make up.

What if you never got a second chance?

It's a good thing that family members and friends almost always forgive one another. They **reconcile**, or come back together in peace.

When we **sin**, we do things that hurt our relationship with God and with others. We need a way to say we are sorry and that we want to do better. We need to ask forgiveness. We want a second chance.

God always loves us. God always offers us forgiveness. We accept God's forgiveness when we are sorry for our sins. We celebrate God's mercy in the Sacrament of **Reconciliation**.

# The Forgiving Father

Jesus told this story to explain the happiness that forgiveness brings.

A man had two sons. The younger son went to his father and said, "Someday everything you have will belong to my brother and me. I want my share now." So the father gave the younger son a lot of money.

The son moved to a faraway city. He spent all his money partying. Soon the son was poor, hungry, and homeless.

The only job the son could get was taking care of a farmer's pigs. He slept in the smelly barn. "These pigs have better food than I do," the son thought. "I should go home. Maybe if I tell my father how sorry I am, he'll let me work as one of his servants."

So the son set out for his home far away. While he was still on the road, the son saw his father running toward him with his arms open. The son fell to his knees. "Forgive me, Father," the son said. "I'm a sinner. I have hurt you and the whole family. I'm so sorry."

Before the son could even finish, the father hugged him joyfully. "Welcome home, my son!" he said. The father gave the son new clothes and threw a party for the whole neighborhood. "Rejoice with me," the father said to everyone. "It was like my son was dead and now he is alive again!"

—based on Luke 15:11–32

# Our Second Chance

Baptism takes away **original sin** and all personal sin. But because we are human, we are tempted to do what is wrong. We have **free will**, like the son in Jesus' story. We can choose to sin. The Sacrament of Reconciliation gives us a chance to ask God's forgiveness and promise to do better.

Baptism, the first sacrament, is a once-in-a-lifetime sacrament. The Sacrament of Reconciliation can be celebrated at any time, again and again throughout our lives. Reconciliation is necessary in the case of serious sin. It is helpful even in the case of less serious sin.

We almost always celebrate Reconciliation in two different ways. In **individual** celebrations a person called a **penitent** meets with a priest in private. In **communal** celebrations groups of people gather to pray and listen to readings from the Bible. Then each person speaks privately with a priest.

Whichever way we celebrate, the priest does not forgive our sins. Only God can forgive sins. The priest acts in the name of Jesus, who shows us God's forgiving love. Like the father in Jesus' story, the priest welcomes us back home to our Catholic community.

### We Ask

**What is the difference between mortal sin and venial sin?**

Serious sin is called **mortal**, or "deadly." It cuts us off from God's grace and friendship. For sin to be mortal, it must be seriously wrong, we must know it is seriously wrong, and we must freely choose to do it anyway. **Venial** sin is less serious, but it still hurts our relationship with God and others. *(Catechism, #1855–1857)*

## Welcome Home

In the heart, draw or write about how it makes you feel to be preparing for your First Reconciliation.

# We Ask God's Blessing

In the Sacrament of Reconciliation, we are all welcomed home by our forgiving Father.

May the Father bless us,
for he has adopted us as his children.
   **Amen!**
May the Son come to help us,
for he has welcomed us as brothers
   and sisters.
   **Amen!**
May the Spirit be with us,
for he has made his home in us.
   **Amen!**

*—based on the Rite of Penance*

# CHAPTER 3
# WE HEAR GOOD NEWS

**D**ear God—Father, Son, and Holy Spirit—you give us the good news of your love. Help us understand your word and live by it. Amen!

What's the best news you have ever heard?

Maybe you found out you were going to have a brother or sister. Maybe your dog had puppies, or you found out your favorite relative was coming to visit for a week.

What did you do when you heard the news? Most people want to tell someone else right away. Good news is meant to be shared.

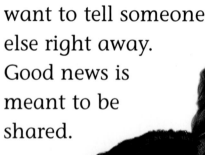

God has good news for us. God our Father sent his Son, Jesus, to bring us the good news of his love and forgiveness. We hear this good news whenever we hear or read the words of **Scripture**, found in the Bible.

God's good news is especially important to share when we are feeling sorry for sin. Readings from the Bible are part of our celebration of the Sacrament of Reconciliation. God's good news gives us the hope and courage we need to start again.

# One Lost Sheep

People sometimes asked Jesus why he spent so much time with sinners. Shouldn't he be bringing the good news of God's love to holy people? Jesus answered them with a story.

Once there was a shepherd who took care of a hundred sheep. Every night before closing the gate to the sheep pen, the shepherd counted his sheep.

One night there were only ninety-nine. The shepherd counted again. Still only ninety-nine! Where could the missing sheep be?

The shepherd called all his friends to help him look. "Why bother?" one friend asked. "It's only one lost sheep. You've got ninety-nine safe here to take care of!"

"It's the one lost sheep who needs me most," the shepherd said. Then he and his friends looked everywhere a wandering sheep might hide. Finally, the shepherd found his one lost sheep. It was curled up under a bush, tired and frightened. The shepherd put the sheep on his shoulders.

He called out to his friends, "Stop searching! I've found the sheep that was lost!"

The shepherd and his friends sang as they brought the lost sheep home. They woke up all ninety-nine other sheep with their shouts of joy!

—based on Luke 15:1–7

# Words of Love and Mercy

Jesus' story about the lost sheep reminds us how much God loves us and wants to forgive us. This story, and many others, can be found in the **Gospels**, the books of the Bible that tell about Jesus' life and teachings. The word **gospel** means "good news."

Readings from the Bible are part of the celebration of every sacrament. We call this the **Celebration of the Word of God.**

We share stories from the Bible as part of the Sacrament of Reconciliation. These words of love and mercy help us see where we have sinned and how we can do better.

In a communal celebration of Reconciliation, we begin by singing a hymn. We pray that God will open our hearts so that we can ask forgiveness. Then we hear one or more readings from the Bible. The priest helps us understand what we have heard.

When we celebrate Reconciliation individually, the priest may read or have us read a few words from the Bible when we first get together. The message of Scripture starts us on our celebration of God's forgiving love.

**We Ask**

**How can we hear God speaking to us?**

Scripture is God's own word. When we hear or read the Bible as part of the Sacrament of Reconciliation, we are hearing God's message for us. In a communal celebration of Reconciliation, the priest's **homily** helps us understand the readings and apply them to our lives. In an individual celebration the priest and the penitent may discuss the Scripture reading together.
*(Catechism, #104, 1349)*

## Words to Live By

Your teacher will write some Bible verses on the board. Choose your favorite, and copy it onto the bookmark.

_____

_____

_____

_____

_____

_____

_____

# The Lord Is Good!

We thank God for the good news of his love.

Shout praises to the LORD, everyone on
    this earth.
Be joyful and sing as you come in to
    worship the LORD!
    **The LORD is good!**
    **His love and faithfulness will last forever.**
You know the LORD is God!
He created us, and we belong to him;
    we are his people, the sheep in his pasture.
    **The LORD is good!**
    **His love and faithfulness will last forever.**
Be thankful and praise the LORD
    as you enter his temple.
    **The LORD is good!**
    **His love and faithfulness will last forever.**

*—Psalm 100*

# CHAPTER 4
# WE LOOK AT OUR LIVES

**D**ear God—Father, Son, and Holy Spirit—
you call us to be happy with you forever.
Help us live by our covenant of love with you.
Amen!

What makes you happy? Real happiness comes
from sharing love, friendship, and good times.
God made each person to be really happy
forever. We are most happy when we are living
the way God made us to live.

God loves us so much. He gave us the **commandments** as a sign of his love. The commandments show us how to live as God wants us to live. They tell us how to love God and others. The commandments show us the way to real happiness.

# The Great Commandment

God made a **covenant**, a lasting promise of love, with the people of Israel. God gave their leader, Moses, the commandments as a sign of the covenant. The Ten Commandments were carved on stone tablets.

But the commandments were not just laws written on stone. The people kept these words in their hearts. They honored them in their lives.

One day when Jesus was teaching in a small town, a man who studied the commandments asked Jesus a question.

"What must I do to be happy forever with God?" he asked.

Jesus answered with a question of his own. "When you study God's law," Jesus asked, "what does it tell you?"

The student smiled. He said, "Love God with all your heart, with all your being, with all your strength, and with all your mind, and love your neighbor as you love yourself."

Jesus smiled, too. "That is the **Great Commandment**!" he said. "Do this, and you will live forever with God."

*—based on Luke 10:25–28*

# How Do We Measure Up?

We know that we do not always live as God wants us to live. We do not always honor the commandments.

When we celebrate the Sacrament of Reconciliation, we look at our lives. We ask the Holy Spirit to help us see where we have made wrong choices.

This prayerful way of looking at our lives is called an **examination of conscience**. We measure our actions against the Ten Commandments, the Beatitudes, the life of Jesus, and the teachings of the Church.

We ask ourselves if we are really happy. We ask, "What would Jesus do?" Are we really living as God wants us to live? Have we failed to show love for God and for others? Have we been selfish or hurtful?

The Holy Spirit will not just help us see where we have gone wrong. God's loving Spirit will also show us how we can do better.

## Signs of Love

Finish the prayer by writing or drawing
in each space.

**Dear God,
I love you. I will
show my love
for you by . . .**

**I love others,
too. I will show
my love for
others by . . .**

# Send Us Your Spirit

**The Holy Spirit helps us do what is right.**

God our Father,
you made the human family
to live with you forever.
> **Send us your Holy Spirit!**
> **Open our hearts to your love!**

Open our ears to your voice
so that we may turn to you
with sorrow for our sins.
> **Send us your Holy Spirit!**
> **Open our hearts to your love!**

Help us grow in your love and grace,
which bring us true happiness,
so that we may live with you forever.
> **Send us your Holy Spirit!**
> **Open our hearts to your love!**

—*adapted from the Rite of Penance*

# CHAPTER 5
# WE ASK FORGIVENESS

Dear God—Father, Son, and Holy Spirit—you call us to make peace when we do wrong. Help us ask forgiveness and do penance. Amen!

Have you ever done something that hurt someone else?

Everyone makes mistakes. Everyone makes wrong choices at some time. When you choose to do something you know is wrong, you sin. Sin is not the same thing as making a mistake.

Sin hurts. It hurts you. It hurts others. Part of healing the hurt is taking **responsibility** for your actions. You admit that you did wrong. Then you do something with God's help to make things right.

The Sacrament of Reconciliation gives us a way to admit that we have done wrong. We **confess** our sins. And the sacrament gives us a way to make things right with God's help. We are given a **penance** to do. Accepting and doing our penance is a sign that we want to grow more loving.

# The Man Who Changed His Life

My name is Zacchaeus. My job is collecting taxes. I've never been very popular because no one likes to pay tax. Also, I'm short, so people sometimes make fun of me. I used to make myself feel better by cheating people. I charged too much tax and kept the extra money for myself.

Then I heard about Jesus, the great teacher. He was very popular. Everybody wanted to see him. I heard he healed people and forgave sins.

One day Jesus came to our town. The crowds were so big I couldn't see, so I climbed a tree. You can imagine how surprised I was when Jesus stopped and looked straight up at me.

"Zacchaeus!" he said, smiling. "Come down! I want to eat lunch at your house today!"

"Me?" I said. "Nobody wants to eat with me!"

"That's right," the people grumbled. "We don't eat with sinners. This man cheats and steals!"

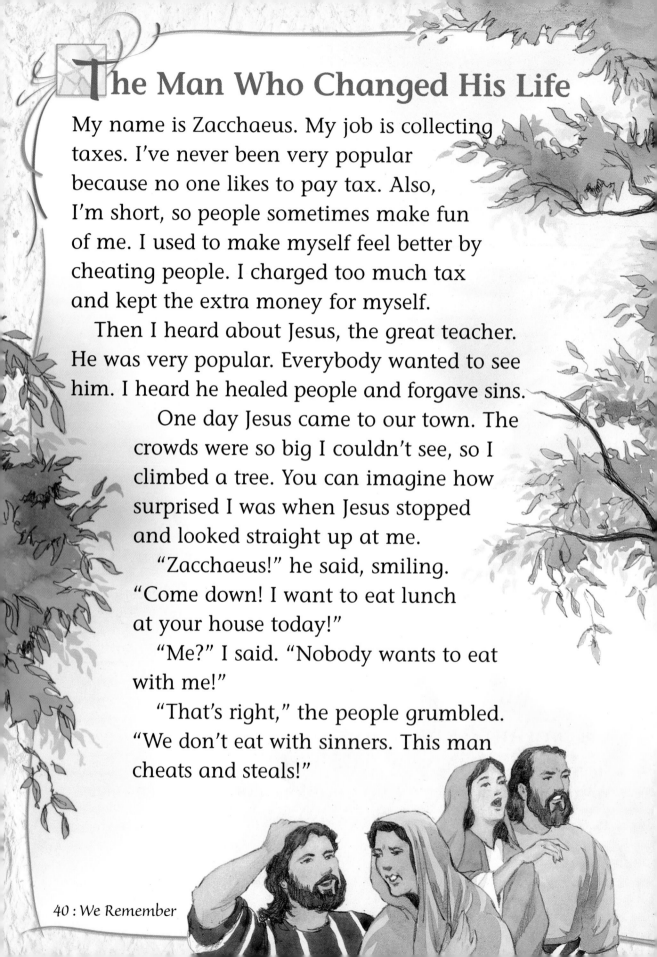

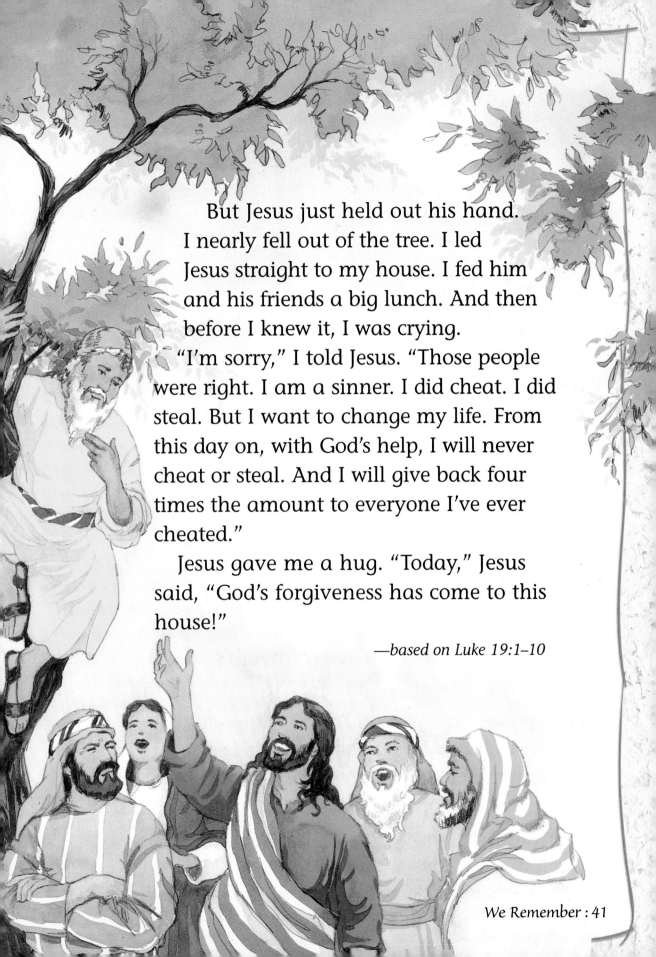

But Jesus just held out his hand. I nearly fell out of the tree. I led Jesus straight to my house. I fed him and his friends a big lunch. And then before I knew it, I was crying.

"I'm sorry," I told Jesus. "Those people were right. I am a sinner. I did cheat. I did steal. But I want to change my life. From this day on, with God's help, I will never cheat or steal. And I will give back four times the amount to everyone I've ever cheated."

Jesus gave me a hug. "Today," Jesus said, "God's forgiveness has come to this house!"

—*based on Luke 19:1–10*

# Confession and Penance

Zacchaeus confessed his sins to Jesus. Then he promised to return four times the amount of money he had stolen.

In the Sacrament of Reconciliation, we do what Zacchaeus did. We confess our sins to the priest, who acts in the name of Jesus. We talk with the priest about how we can make things right.

The priest gives us a penance to do. The penance may be to spend some time praying. Or it may be an action connected to the sin, such as returning stolen property or helping repair something broken.

Doing penance helps us take responsibility for our actions. It reminds us to think twice about how our choices might hurt others. Penance is not punishment. It is a way to learn and grow more loving. Penance is so important that our celebration of the Sacrament of Reconciliation is called the **Rite of Penance**.

Whether we celebrate Reconciliation individually or communally, confession and the giving of a penance almost always take place privately between the penitent and the priest.

## We Ask

**Why do we confess our sins to a priest?**

Confessing our sins aloud helps us take responsibility for our actions. Only God forgives sin, but the priest acts as God's minister by listening to our confession, giving us a penance, and encouraging us to avoid sin in the future. The priest may never tell anyone what he hears in confession. *(Catechism, #1455–1456, 1467)*

## I Do Penance

On one side of the vase, draw or write about a wrong choice. On the other side, draw or write about something that will make things right with God's help.

I'm Sorry I am so

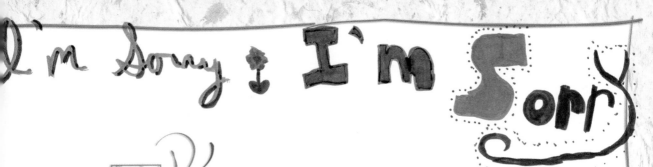
## God Loves Us

We admit that we have done wrong. But
we accept God's forgiveness when we show
sorrow and promise to do better.

God our Father,
sometimes we have not behaved as your
   children should.
   **But you love us and come to us.**
We have quarreled.
We have been lazy.
   **But you love us and come to us.**
We have not been helpful.
We have not done good to others
when we had the chance.
   **But you love us and come to us.**
With Jesus our Brother
we come before you
and ask you to forgive our sins.
   **Amen!**

*—based on the Rite of Penance*

I'm Sorry

# CHAPTER 6
# WE GO FORTH IN PARDON AND PEACE

Dear God—Father, Son, and Holy Spirit—
you free us from sin when we are sorry.
Help us grow in peace and love.
Amen!

How do you show someone you are sorry?

You can use words. You can use gestures, like a hug or a handshake. Sometimes tears are a sign that you are sorry.

What do you want to happen when you say you are sorry?

In the Sacrament of Reconciliation, we show sorrow for sin by praying an **Act of Contrition**. In the prayer we tell God how sorry we are for having sinned. We promise to do better.

When we say we are sorry, we want our wrong choices to be forgiven. And we want the chance to start over.

In the Sacrament of Reconciliation, we celebrate God's forgiveness. In the name of God and the Church, the priest gives us **absolution**. We start fresh, with joy.

# The Forgiven Woman

I knew everyone was looking at me. After all, I was known all over town as a terrible sinner. No one had invited me to this banquet at the house of Simon, a holy man.

But I had to see Jesus. I had to let him know that I wasn't a sinner anymore. I had been given the great gift of God's loving forgiveness.

I couldn't help it. As soon as I saw Jesus, I fell down before him. My tears washed the dust from his feet. My hair dried them. Then I poured sweet perfumed oil on his feet. The jar had cost me everything I had in the world, but it was worth it.

"I know what you're thinking, Simon," Jesus said to his shocked host. "How can I let this great sinner anywhere near me? But I can tell by her tears and her love that she has been forgiven."

"Yes, but . . ." Simon sputtered.

"Think of it this way," Jesus said. "What if two people owe you money—one a lot and one a little. You tell both of them they don't have to pay. Which one is going to be more grateful?"

Simon began to understand. "The person who has been forgiven more will be happier," he said.

"This woman has done more for me than you did," Jesus said. "That's how I know how much she has been forgiven."

Jesus looked at me with kindness. "Your sins are forgiven," he said. "Now go in peace." As I walked out of Simon's great hall with everyone's eyes on me, I held my head up. I felt like dancing.

*—based on Luke 7:36–50*

# Contrition and Absolution

Contrition, or sorrow for sin, is necessary for accepting God's forgiveness. In the Sacrament of Reconciliation, we show contrition in the words of a prayer. There are many versions of the Act of Contrition, but each one says the same thing. We have sinned. We are sorry. We ask God's forgiveness. We promise to do better.

In a communal celebration of the sacrament, our prayer of contrition is followed by a **litany** spoken by the whole group. The Lord's Prayer always concludes the litany. In individual celebrations, the penitent prays an Act of Contrition after confessing and receiving a penance.

The Sacrament of Reconciliation almost always includes private absolution of the penitent by the priest. Holding out his hand as a sign of the Holy Spirit's blessing, the priest prays, "Through the ministry of the Church, may God give you **pardon** and peace, and I absolve you from your sins in the name of the Father, and of the Son, and of the Holy Spirit." We answer, "Amen."

Our celebration almost always ends with a joyful song or prayer of thanks to God. Like the woman whom Jesus forgave, we are overflowing with gratitude for God's love and mercy. We go forth in peace.

**We Ask**

**What does the Sacrament of Reconciliation do for us?**

The Sacrament of Reconciliation does exactly what its name describes. Through sacramental confession and absolution, we are **reconciled**, or brought back together, with God. That reconciliation has other effects. We are reconciled with our own conscience, allowing us to feel inner peace. We are reconciled with others, especially those whom we have hurt. We are reconciled with the Christian community, making the whole Church stronger. And we are reconciled with all God's creation. (Catechism, #1469)

## I Promise to Do Better

On the lines, write your own Act of Contrition. Then decorate the frame with joyful colors.

_____

_____

_____

_____

_____

_____

_____

# Thank You, God!

We thank God for the Sacrament of Reconciliation.

God and Father of us all,
you have forgiven our sins.
**Thank you for your mercy!**
You have given us your peace.
**Thank you for your peace!**
Help us forgive one another.
**Help us show mercy.**
Help us work together for peace
in the world.
**Help us share peace.**
**Amen!**

*—based on the Rite of Penance*

# Catholic Prayers

## The Sign of the Cross

In the name of the Father,
and of the Son,
and of the Holy Spirit.
Amen.

## The Lord's Prayer

Our Father, who art in heaven,
hallowed be thy name;
thy kingdom come;
thy will be done on earth as it is in heaven.
Give us this day our daily bread;
and forgive us our trespasses
as we forgive those who trespass against us;
and lead us not into temptation,
but deliver us from evil.
Amen.

## Hail Mary

Hail, Mary, full of grace,
the Lord is with you!
Blessed are you among women,
and blessed is the fruit of your womb, Jesus.
Holy Mary, Mother of God,
pray for us sinners,
now and at the hour of our death.
Amen.

## Glory to the Father (Doxology)

Glory to the Father,
and to the Son,
and to the Holy Spirit,
as it was in the beginning,
is now, and will be for ever.
Amen.

## I Confess (Confiteor)

I confess to almighty God,
and to you, my brothers and sisters,
that I have sinned through my own fault
in my thoughts and in my words,
in what I have done,
and in what I have failed to do;
and I ask blessed Mary, ever virgin,
all the angels and saints,
and you, my brothers and sisters,
to pray for me to the Lord our God.

## Act of Contrition

My God,
I am sorry for my sins with all my heart.
In choosing to do wrong
and failing to do good,
I have sinned against you
whom I should love above all things.
I firmly intend, with your help,
to do penance,
to sin no more,
and to avoid whatever leads me to sin.
Our Savior Jesus Christ
suffered and died for us.
In his name, my God, have mercy.

## The Jesus Prayer

Lord Jesus, Son of God,
have mercy on me, a sinner.
Amen.

# Our Moral Guide

## The Great Commandment

"You shall love the Lord your God with all your heart,
with all your soul, with all your strength, and with all
  your mind;
and your neighbor as yourself."

—*Luke 10:27*


## The Beatitudes

"Blessed are the poor in spirit,
    for theirs is the kingdom of heaven.
Blessed are they who mourn,
    for they will be comforted.
Blessed are the meek,
    for they will inherit the land.
Blessed are they who hunger and thirst for
righteousness,
    for they will be satisfied.
Blessed are the merciful,
    for they will be shown mercy.
Blessed are the clean of heart,
    for they will see God.
Blessed are the peacemakers,
    for they will be called children of God.
Blessed are they who are persecuted for the sake of
righteousness,
    for theirs is the kingdom of heaven."

—*Matthew 5:3–10*

# The Ten Commandments

1. **I am the Lord your God. You shall not have strange gods before me.**
   Put God first in your life before all things.

2. **You shall not take the name of the Lord your God in vain.**
   Respect God's name and holy things. Do not use bad language.

3. **Remember to keep holy the Lord's day.**
   Take part in the Mass on Sundays and holy days. Avoid unnecessary work on these days.

4. **Honor your father and your mother.**
   Obey and show respect to parents and others who are responsible for you.

5. **You shall not kill.**
   Do not hurt yourself or others. Take care of all life.

6. **You shall not commit adultery.**
   Show respect for marriage and family life. Respect your body and the bodies of others.

7. **You shall not steal.**
   Respect creation and the things that belong to others. Do not cheat.

8. **You shall not bear false witness against your neighbor.**
   Tell the truth. Do not gossip.

9. **You shall not covet your neighbor's wife.**
   Be faithful to family members and friends. Do not be jealous.

10. **You shall not covet your neighbor's goods.**
    Share what you have. Do not envy what other people have. Do not be greedy.

## Precepts of the Church

1. Take part in the Mass on Sundays and holy days. Keep these days holy, and avoid unnecessary work.
2. Celebrate the Sacrament of Reconciliation at least once a year if there is serious sin.
3. Receive Holy Communion at least once a year during Easter time.
4. Fast and abstain on days of penance.
5. Give your time, gifts, and money to support the Church.

## Works of Mercy

**Corporal (for the body)**

Feed the hungry.

Give drink to the thirsty.

Clothe the naked.

Shelter the homeless.

Visit the sick.

Visit the imprisoned.

Bury the dead.

**Spiritual (for the spirit)**

Warn the sinner.

Teach the ignorant.

Counsel the doubtful.

Comfort the sorrowful.

Bear wrongs patiently.

Forgive injuries.

Pray for the living and the dead.

# Examination of Conscience

1. Look at your life. Compare your actions and choices with the Beatitudes, the Ten Commandments, the Great Commandment, and the precepts of the Church.
2. Ask yourself:
   - When have I not done what God wants me to do?
   - Whom have I hurt?
   - What have I done that I knew was wrong?
   - What have I not done that I should have done?
   - Are there serious sins I did not mention the last time I confessed?
   - Have I done penance? Have I tried as hard as I could to make up for past sins?
   - Have I changed my bad habits?
   - Am I sincerely sorry for all my sins?
3. In addition to confessing your sins, you may want to talk to the priest about one or more of the above questions.
4. Pray for the Holy Spirit's help to change and start over.

# Celebrating the Sacrament of Reconciliation

## The Communal Rite of Reconciliation

- Before celebrating the Sacrament of Reconciliation, take time to examine your conscience. Pray for the Holy Spirit's help.

1. **Introductory Rites**
   Join in singing the opening hymn. The priest will greet the assembly and lead you in the opening prayer.

2. **Reading from Scripture**
   Listen to the word of God. There may be more than one reading, with a hymn or psalm in between. The last reading will be from one of the Gospels.

3. **Homily**
   Listen as the priest helps you understand the meaning of the Scriptures.

4. **Examination of Conscience with Litany of Contrition and the Lord's Prayer**
   After the homily there will be a time of silence. The priest may lead the assembly in an examination of conscience. This is followed by the prayer of confession and the litany or song. Then all will pray the Lord's Prayer together.

5. **Individual Confession, Giving of Penance, and Absolution**
   While you wait your turn to talk with the priest, you may pray quietly or join in singing. When it is your turn, confess your sins to the priest. He will talk to you about how to do better and give you a penance. Then the priest will pray the prayer of absolution.

6. **Closing Rite**
   After everyone has confessed individually, join in singing or praying a song or litany of thanksgiving. The priest will lead the closing prayer and bless the assembly. Then the priest or deacon will dismiss the assembly.

- After celebrating the sacrament, carry out your penance as soon as possible.

# The Individual Rite of Reconciliation

- Before celebrating the Sacrament of Reconciliation, take time to examine your conscience. Pray for the Holy Spirit's help.
- Wait for your turn to enter the Reconciliation room.
- You may meet with the priest face-to-face or be separated from the priest by a screen.

1. **Welcome**
   The priest will welcome you and invite you to pray the Sign of the Cross.

2. **Reading from Scripture**
   The priest may read or recite a passage from the Bible. You may be invited by the priest to read the Scripture yourself.

3. **Confession of Sins and Giving of Penance**
   Tell your sins to the priest. The priest will talk with you about how to do better. Then the priest will give you a penance.

4. **Act of Contrition**
   Pray an Act of Contrition.

5. **Absolution**
   The priest will hold his hand over your head and pray the prayer of absolution. As he says the final words, he will make the Sign of the Cross.

6. **Closing Prayer**
   The priest will pray, "Give thanks to the Lord, for he is good." You answer, "His mercy endures for ever." Then the priest will dismiss you.

- After celebrating the sacrament, carry out your penance as soon as possible.

# Illustrated Glossary

## absolution

(ab•suh•LOO•shuhn): The forgiveness of sin we receive from God through the Church in the Sacrament of Reconciliation. The word *absolve* means "to wash away."

## communal celebration

(kuh•MYOO•nuhl seh•luh•BRAY•shuhn): One form of celebrating the Sacrament of Reconciliation. In a communal celebration the assembly gathers to pray and hear God's word. Each penitent then confesses, receives a penance, and is absolved privately.

## confession

(kuhn•FEH•shuhn): Telling our sins to a priest in the Sacrament of Reconciliation. What we confess to the priest is private.

## contrition

(kuhn•TRIH•shuhn): Sorrow for sins and a willingness to do better. Contrition is our first step toward forgiveness. As part of the Sacrament of Reconciliation, we pray an **Act**, or Prayer, **of Contrition**.

## examination of conscience
(ig•ZA•muh•NAY•shuhn UHV KAHNT•shuhnts):
A prayerful way of looking at our lives in light of the Ten Commandments, the Beatitudes, the life of Jesus, and the teachings of the Church.

## individual celebration
(in•duh•VIJ•wuhl seh•luh•BRAY•shuhn): One form of celebrating the Sacrament of Reconciliation. In an individual celebration the penitent meets with the priest in private. The penitent then confesses, receives a penance, and is absolved privately.

## penance
(PEH•nuhnts): Prayers and actions done to make up for the harm our sins have caused. In the Sacrament of Reconciliation, the priest gives us a penance to do. The celebration of the Sacrament of Reconciliation is called the **Rite of Penance.**

## penitent
(PEH•nuh•tuhnt): The person who confesses his or her sins to the priest in the Sacrament of Reconciliation.

## priest

(PREEST): A man who is ordained to serve God and the Church by celebrating the sacraments, preaching, and presiding at Mass. The priest is the **confessor**, or minister of the Sacrament of Reconciliation. For the Sacrament of Reconciliation, the priest wears a stole. The **stole** is a sign of the priest's obedience to God and of his priestly authority.

## Reconciliation room

(REH•kuhn•sih•lee•AY•shuhn ROOM): A room or chapel in which the confessor hears the penitent's confession of sins. The room is usually furnished with chairs, a kneeler, a table for the Bible and candle, and a movable screen that can be used as a divider between the priest and the penitent.

## Scripture

(SKRIPT•sher): The word of God contained in the Bible. The word *scripture* means "holy writing." Scripture is used for reflecting on God's love and forgiveness in the Sacrament of Reconciliation. Scripture is proclaimed by a **lector**, or reader, at Mass or in other liturgical celebrations.

## sin

(SIN): The choice to disobey God. Sin can be serious (**mortal**) or less serious (**venial**). Sin is a deliberate choice, not a mistake or an accident. We accept God's loving forgiveness for our sins when we show by our sorrow that we are willing to do better.